THE
MINDFULNESS
COMPANION

A CREATIVE JOURNAL TO BRING CALM TO YOUR DAY

DR SARAH JANE ARNOLD

WITH ILLUSTRATIONS BY ANGELEA VAN DAM

Michael O'Mara Books Limited

First published in Great Britain in 2016 by
Michael O'Mara Books Limited
9 Lion Yard
Tremadoc Road
London SW4 7NQ

A CIP catalogue record for this book is available from the British Library.

Papers used by Michael O'Mara Books Limited are natural, recyclable
products made from wood grown in sustainable forests. The manufacturing
processes conform to the environmental regulations of the country of origin.

ISBN: 978-1-78243-581-5 in paperback print format

5 6 7 8 9 10

www.mombooks.com

Cover and interior illustrations by Angelea Van Dam
Cover design by Ana Bjezancevic
Designed and typeset by Claire Cater

Every reasonable effort has been made to acknowledge all copyright holders.
Any errors or omissions that may have occurred are inadvertent, and anyone
with any copyright queries is invited to write to the publisher, so that full
acknowledgement may be included in subsequent editions of the work.

Printed and bound in China

Introducing Mindfulness

Modern life can be busy and demanding. To cope, we plan, strive, work towards our goals, attend to multiple things at once, and go on autopilot to conserve our mental energy and attend to our priorities. This 'doing mode' is helpful and positive for us in many respects. It can enable us to progress and achieve the things that we want to do. It is a source of self-esteem. However, *doing* is also associated with the desire for change, dissatisfaction with how things are now, pressure and expectations, the unconscious mind and learned behaviours. We can be unhelpfully influenced by negative thoughts and challenging feelings when our minds are on autopilot. We may feel drained and incomplete, and forget to appreciate all that we are and all that we have *right now*. Mindfulness offers an accessible way of managing these issues, so that you can achieve a more healthy balance between 'doing' and 'being' in life.

Mindfulness draws on ancient concepts from Buddhist teachings that are associated with well-being. Simply put, mindfulness means deliberately paying full attention to the present moment, with an attitude of acceptance, kindness, compassion, openness and curiosity. It is about being in the now, rather than doing for the future. The practice of mindfulness offers you an alternative way of relating to your external world (your relationships and environment) and your internal experiences (your thoughts, feelings and bodily sensations) without unhelpful judgements or kneejerk reactions that can cause distress.

Why Do It?

Western science and psychology have adopted mindfulness because research has found strong evidence that it significantly enhances well-being. For example, mindfulness-based psychological therapy has been found to successfully relieve anxiety disorders, depression and stress. There is evidence, too, suggesting that mindfulness can be helpful for some people with physical health concerns, such as chronic pain.

It is understood that mindfulness is beneficial for several reasons:

1. Mindfulness encourages you to accept and tolerate challenging emotions, and teaches you not to react in unhelpful ways. A great deal of psychological distress is associated with people trying to suppress or avoid their emotions.
2. Mindfulness supports you to change unhelpful, automatic

patterns of thinking and behaving. When you practise mindful living in the present, your mind dwells less in the past (an aspect of depression) and it gets less caught up in concerns about the future (a feature of anxiety). You learn to view your thoughts as *just thoughts* (that may or may not be true), which you observe from a distance as they enter, stay and leave your mind. You can then choose if, how and when you want to respond to them with a more balanced and self-aware mindset.

3. Mindfulness encourages you to be more kind and compassionate to yourself and others. A significant proportion of emotional pain is associated with self-critical thoughts, unhelpful expectations and difficult relationship dynamics.

4. Mindfulness can help you to feel more relaxed and at peace, and accepting of who you are – just as you are. It can promote a sense of appreciation for life and remind you of its wondrous qualities.

It is important to note that you are not aiming for these outcomes while practising mindfulness; mindfulness is not about striving or wishing that things were different from how they are. However, a positive consequence of practising mindfulness is that people often find that their well-being increases.

How Do You Do It?

Mindfulness involves learning how to pay attention to your immediate experience of the present moment, just as it is, right now. In order to do this, you can focus on the experience of yourself breathing, your body and bodily sensations, your thoughts and/or your emotions. You can also focus your attention on your external world, such as what you can see, hear, touch, taste and smell, moment by moment. Mindfulness is a process of observing, noticing, allowing and becoming aware of these things, without judging, evaluating or trying to change your experiences. Mindfulness is also a way of being. When you are being mindful, you take a stance of openness, curiosity, non-judgement and non-reactivity, and you accept your experiences – just as they are. You may notice that your mind tells you that you do not like some of your experiences, but when practising mindfulness you accept them, nonetheless, as part of your reality in that moment. When you are being mindful, you also take a stance of self-compassion, and of compassion and loving-kindness towards others. When you feel compassion in this way, you are wishing that you and others are free from suffering. When you feel loving-kindness, you are wishing that you and others are safe, well and happy, and you extend this love and kindness to all living beings.

You can practise mindfulness formally and/or informally. Formal mindfulness meditation is when you intentionally take time out from your day, find a quiet space, and then practise mindfulness for a certain amount of time. You typically sit in a comfortable upright position when you meditate, although some formal meditations ask you to lie down. It is usual to close your eyes when you practise formal meditation, to help you focus, and to use a clock to keep time. Many people find that it is best to start small. For example, you could begin with a simple three-minute meditation. You could then slowly increase it to five, ten or fifteen minutes. When it becomes familiar, you may choose to pursue a sustained meditation for a longer period of time, say, up to one hour. It can be useful to follow a guided meditation recording at first, to help you become more familiar with what mindfulness is and how to do it.

Informal mindfulness practice, by contrast, is when you engage with your daily activities in a mindful way. You may be on the bus, cooking, eating or walking mindfully, for example. You do not need to take time out to do this, and you do not need to close your eyes. On the contrary, informal mindful awareness can be practised whatever you are doing, anywhere and at any time that suits you. You can be informally mindful for as long as you want to.

Mindfulness is a natural human ability that can be cultivated with guidance, practice, trust and patience. It may seem simple, but many people find that it is not easy. You may find it hard to hold the focus of your attention, or you may question whether you are 'doing it right', and your mind may be easily distracted. Pay attention to how you respond to yourself in such moments. There is no need to criticize yourself or judge your experience negatively. Mindfulness is a skill, and, like any new skill, it takes practice to cultivate. Remind yourself that you are paying attention to the present moment as best you can, and practise attending to yourself and your experiences with an attitude of kindness and curiosity instead. With time, the skill and art of mindfulness can become a new way of relating to yourself and your environment. It can be incorporated into your daily life as much or as little as you like.

Mindfulness and Colouring

Colouring is one enjoyable, creative way of incorporating mindfulness into your life. Naturally, colouring, drawing, painting and other creative pursuits have a great deal in common with mindfulness meditation. Like mindfulness, they too involve awareness, making conscious choices, finding focus, connecting with the body, curiosity, going with the flow and becoming absorbed in an activity with a childlike ease of being. They can evoke feelings of living in the now, simply being, enjoyment, fulfilment and calm. They can also activate our expectations and critical judgements, which can be managed effectively with a mindful mind.

This book offers you an introduction to some of the fundamental principles of mindfulness. It also provides the opportunity to practise mindfulness via colouring. Each page of colouring is accompanied by an exercise that will enhance your understanding of what mindfulness is and how to do it. Some of the exercises will assist specifically with your experience of mindful colouring. Others will teach you more general mindfulness skills that you can practise before or while you are colouring. There are also inspirational quotes, 'mindful moments' that can be used like mantras, and spaces to write your thoughts and feelings. Ultimately, this book is designed to promote your well-being. It is your companion, to help you harness your creativity, express yourself in colour, and live mindfully – moment by moment.

With warm wishes,
Dr Sarah Jane Arnold

WR1 2.2

Burn			Faster			Stronger		
86	111	117	22	23	24	36	52	62
104	90	100		41	56	35	49	52
54	80	103	11	15	14	10	14	15

Powerful			Cut			Balanced		
10	16	14	55	72	74	10	8	24
61?	9	11	17	21	24	8	16	27
34	42	50	14	18	22	9	18	19

Burn			Faster			Stronger		
124	115	120	26	25	27	68	62	53
114	106	111	60	61	60	55	61	68
110	109	115	16	19	20	55	61	68

26 lunch bance 120

Powerful			Cut				Balanced			17
21	21	35	76	97	73	83	28	36	35	
15	12	12	25	21	25	26 30	30	39	41	
54	56	34	28	30	10 40 36	21	23	26		

Cut 1		Cut 2		117	25		Cut 3	
51	54	51		67	12		51	55
	23		22	89	70		30	2?
41	45		37				44	50

31 - XL   24 - XXL
- 5 Groucho   - 2 - Balmore
- 3 - Balmore

28 - M   54 - L
                 - 5 - Groucho
                 - 2 - AC
Box of Juniors   - 2 - NCR
_____↗_____

155 +

'The art of living lies in
a fine mingling of letting
go and holding on.'

Havelock Ellis

Enabling Mindfulness

Notice your intention to colour, and really
look at the patterns that you see. How are
you feeling in this moment? How does your
body feel right now? Take a moment to notice
your posture. Observe your thoughts.
When you decide to colour, see if you can do so
with your full attention, and with a kind, curious
and non-judgemental attitude. Every time you
choose to colour in this way, you are offering
your mind a sanctuary called mindfulness. By
practising mindfulness, you have the opportunity
to experience each moment in your life more fully.
You can begin this experience right now.

Cultivating Gratitude

Gratitude, like mindfulness, involves paying attention to what is present with an attitude of loving-kindness. Can you bring to mind someone or something that you are grateful for? Take your time. It may be an aspect of yourself, like your eyesight. It could be someone present and positive in your life, like a partner, parent or friend. You might think of an aspect of your life, such as where you live. Write down what comes to mind in the space provided in the pattern opposite, and rest in the warmth of this feeling for a while. Begin to colour when you wish, and allow gratitude to be with you.

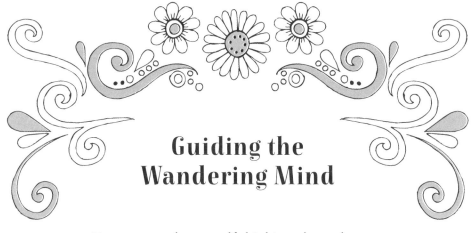

Guiding the Wandering Mind

You may catch yourself thinking about the past or the future when you are colouring, and your mind may flit from thought to thought. If this happens, there is no need to judge yourself – we can be easily distracted. Simply notice where your mind has gone and bring the focus of your attention back to the present moment. Focus on an aspect of your experience right now, and allow it to take centre stage in your awareness. For example, you could look at the piece you are colouring, and pay attention to your breathing. With kindness to yourself, repeat this exercise whenever your mind wanders.

A Mindful Moment

I can observe and
guide my mind.

Reflections:

Embrace Your Pace

Take this opportunity to play mindfully with
the speed of your colouring. Experiment!
Colour very, very slowly for a few minutes,
and then colour incredibly fast. Allow
yourself to be curious. Notice as any thoughts
arise in your mind about this experience.
Observe them, and then let them go.
Now, colour at a pace that feels comfortable
for you. Tune in to yourself and simply
go with the flow. Become aware of how it
feels for you to move at your own pace.
Embrace this way of being right now.

Cultivating Curiosity

As you colour, practise 'pressing pause' at
various points. Do this at least several times
and exercise your instinctual curiosity in the
moments that follow. Pause to look around you
and absorb what your senses are experiencing.
Pause again to notice the colours that you are
using. Consider their shade and tone, and look
at them intently. Notice the position of your
dominant hand and how it feels where it rests.
What will it feel like to sit somewhere
else and colour the rest of this pattern?
Try it, and observe your experience.
Marvel at the richness of any given moment
when you pause to notice what exists.

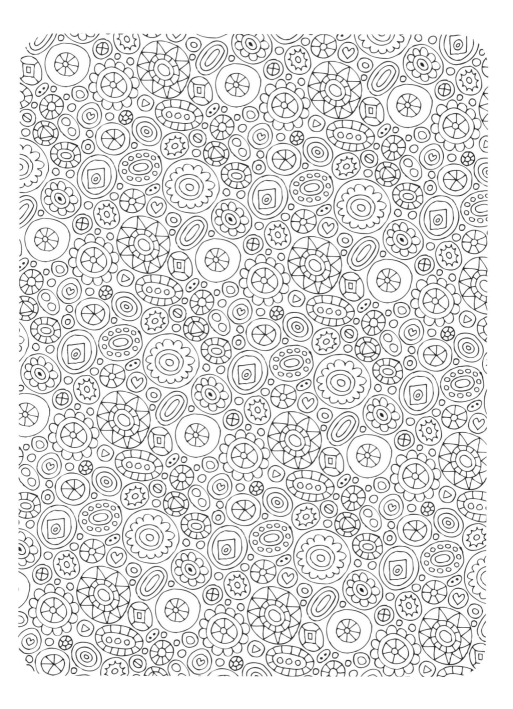

'Knowing yourself is the beginning of all wisdom.'

Aristotle

Mindful Breathing

Before you begin to colour, pay attention to
yourself breathing in this moment. See if you
can breathe gently, in and out. Sit comfortably
and close your eyes for a moment. Allow your
full attention to be directed to your breathing.
Become aware of how the air feels as it passes
in and out through your nose or mouth. Notice
its temperature and any scents in the air. Notice
how it fills your lungs and your chest as you
breathe. Now, open your eyes and begin to
colour when you wish. Breathe in the vitality
of the present moment while you colour.

A Mindful Moment

Breathe in the now.

Mindful Colouring
With Music

Take this time for yourself and put on some of your
favourite music. It may be one song, an album, or
a playlist that will last for hours. When you are
ready to colour and are sitting comfortably, press
play. As you colour, welcome the music into your
body and mind. Allow it to flow through you like
the colour flows from the end of your coloured
pencil or pen. Notice the details and richness
in the music that you are listening to and in the
design that you can see. Maybe write down some
of the lyrics that stand out to you. Your senses are
alive in this moment. Simply go with the flow.

Colour Your Emotions

Take a moment and check in with yourself before
you colour the pattern opposite. What emotions
are you currently feeling? Do you have colours
that represent these emotions? If you do, perhaps
you could use these colours and create with them.
Welcome each emotion that you are feeling just as
you welcome each new colour onto the page, and
simply see what arises. Look upon your creation
with curiosity, compassion and loving-kindness,
and practise accepting each and every emotion
that you notice. This is your experience right now,
and you are allowed to feel the way that you do.

'Be curious, not judgemental.'

Walt Whitman

Self-compassion

See if you can bring to mind the name of a person or a pet that you care about and who cares about you. This is a being that brings you joy. Rest your mind in this place of compassion and loving-kindness for a minute or two, and then write their name within the space opposite. See if you can make room for these feelings while you colour, and then offer yourself this love and kindness. You are important and worthy of such affection too.

A Mindful Moment

Rest in compassion.

Mandala Meditation

Focus your attention and affection on the
mandala before you. Breathe gently, in and out,
and observe its centre, symmetry and intricacies.
Colour at your own pace and welcome the image
of the mandala into your mind. Notice how
interconnected the lines are. Each part has its
place and connection with the other parts. Each
part adds something to the picture to make it
whole. Like you, it is beautifully multifaceted.
As you infuse your mandala with colour, allow
your mind to rest in this sense of wholeness
and connection. Welcome all the different
parts of yourself and express them in colour.

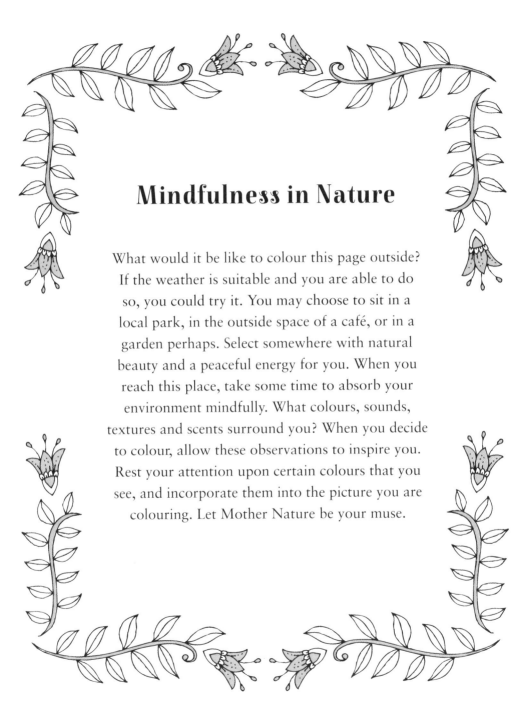

Mindfulness in Nature

What would it be like to colour this page outside?
If the weather is suitable and you are able to do
so, you could try it. You may choose to sit in a
local park, in the outside space of a café, or in a
garden perhaps. Select somewhere with natural
beauty and a peaceful energy for you. When you
reach this place, take some time to absorb your
environment mindfully. What colours, sounds,
textures and scents surround you? When you decide
to colour, allow these observations to inspire you.
Rest your attention upon certain colours that you
see, and incorporate them into the picture you are
colouring. Let Mother Nature be your muse.

'The art of being wise is
knowing what to overlook.'

William James

A Non-judgemental Attitude

While you are colouring, take a moment to pause and observe the picture before you. Notice the colours you have chosen and the aspects of the pattern that your mind is drawn to. Allow the picture to be just as it is, without wanting or needing things to be different. If you notice critical or judgemental thoughts, this is not a problem. Simply recognize that they have come into your mind, and then return your attention to the present moment, to the shapes and colours that you can see, and your breath as you breathe in and out. With kindness and respect, simply observe what lies before you in this moment.

A Mindful Moment

I can choose how I respond
to my thoughts.

Set Your Intention

Create the intention to colour this picture in
a pleasant, warm and relaxing environment.
Consciously carve out this time for yourself,
and select a space that is quiet and peaceful.
You may wish to gather items like incense,
candles, a soft cushion and a blanket for your
comfort. Perhaps put on some soothing music
to enhance the tranquillity of your space.
Create your setting and remind yourself of the
reason behind this: *I deserve this time, to relax
and care for myself.* Hold this kindness and
warmth with you while you colour mindfully.

Extending Compassion and Loving-kindness

Take this opportunity to be silently mindful about someone that you care for deeply. Bring to mind three things that you like about them. Write them down if you wish, and then take some time to appreciate this person's presence in your life. Consider the faces of strangers, and see if you can extend the warmth that you feel for your loved ones to these people too. We were all unknown to each other once.
As you colour the mandala before you, imagine the compassion you feel extending to all living beings. Feel loving-kindness expand with the colours that you add to the page.

May we all be happy, safe and free from suffering.

'When a painful or even a pleasant feeling arises, the Truth is – it is there. Any resistance, trying to control, wishing it away with thoughts, or fighting that feeling in any way, only causes more suffering to arise.'

The Venerable U Vimalaramsi

Cultivating Acceptance

How are you feeling in this moment? Use one word
to describe each emotion that you are experiencing
– for example, 'thoughtful', 'concerned' and
'hopeful' – and write them in the space provided in
the pattern opposite. See if you can make room for
these feelings to be, just as they are. Simply name
them and acknowledge that they are there. You do
not need to like them. Remind yourself that you are
allowed to feel this way, even if it is uncomfortable.
Now, see if you can shift the focus of your attention
to the pattern before you, and colour when you
wish. This moment is meaningful and it is yours.

Reflections:

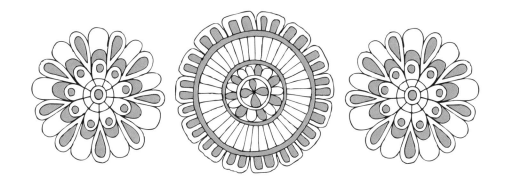

A Mindful Moment

I can tolerate the
emotions that I feel.

Coming Home
to Yourself

Close your eyes and gently bring the focus of your
attention to the centre of your forehead. Allow
your eyes to rest in this direction – in this safety,
in this place – as you breathe gently in and out at
your own pace. Just breathe. This is your sanctuary.
You are coming home to yourself, moment by
moment, with every breath. If your mind wanders,
notice this with kindness and simply refocus your
attention back to the centre of your forehead,
with your eyes closed. Keep breathing mindfully.
Notice how you feel when you decide to open
your eyes, and begin to colour when you wish.

Release

Before you colour, hold both of your hands out
before you and squeeze them as tightly as you
can. Hold them tensed in this position for three
seconds, and then release them. Now do it again.
Clench your fists, and then release. Notice the
tension leaving your body when your hands
open. Let it go, and welcome how your hands feel
without it. Allow any tension to flow out through
your hands as you colour. Release it. There is
no need to hold it with you in this moment.

'The real voyage of
discovery consists not in
seeking new landscapes,
but in having new eyes.'

Marcel Proust

Direct Your Attention Outside

Consciously direct your attention to the
environment that surrounds you right now, and
tune in to the various things that you can see,
hear, touch, taste and smell before you begin to
colour. Notice life's finer details and name the
things that you can perceive, without judgement.
Notice how flexible your attention can be as
you move your focus from one event to the next
at your own pace. Moment by moment, you
are living in the present and experiencing its
fullness – just as it is. It is yours to embrace.

I am deeply connected with
my external world.

Colour With Kindness

Repeat these words to yourself and
see if you can truly mean them.

In this moment, I am good enough.
In this moment, I am lovable.
In this moment, I care for myself.

Write down these words if you want
to, and make space for them to be here
with you now while you colour.

Focus With Curiosity and Patience

What is it like to try to colour with your non-dominant hand? That is, the opposite hand from the one you usually use. See if you can use this hand only, and focus your attention on colouring in this way. Notice how much patience and concentration it requires. It may feel very new and unfamiliar. It may even feel frustrating. Notice and name any emotions that arise, moment by moment, and allow them to be here with you as you try to guide your hand as it colours. See if you can experience this without making any judgements. Notice how present you are in this moment.

'I can alter my life by altering my attitude. He who would have nothing to do with thorns must never attempt to gather flowers.'

Henry David Thoreau

Direct Your Attention Inside

Are there any sensations within you right now? Any thoughts or feelings that you can identify? Practise noticing and naming any emotions and sensations that you feel in this moment, before you begin to colour. Acknowledge your thoughts as thoughts by recognizing them and saying to yourself, 'I'm having a thought that ...' Then return your attention to your breathing, and begin to colour when you wish. In this mindful moment, you can view your internal landscape from a distance with clarity. There is space for you to breathe here. You can see as far as the horizon.

My internal experiences
do not control me. I am
their observer.

In a Challenging Moment ...

Save this exercise for a moment when you
are feeling emotionally challenged.

*In this moment, I can name and allow the emotions
that I am feeling.* Go ahead, write them down.

_____

_____

_____

*In this moment, I can observe the thoughts running
through my mind.* Write these down, too.

_____

_____

_____

*I am grounded in knowing myself and
my struggle in this moment.
I am human, and I care. I am allowed to feel this way.*

*I will ride these waves as they rise and
fall on this ground of mine.
I will refocus my attention when I want
to and colour mindfully.*

I can cope with this. It will pass.

Mindfulness of Sight

What can you see right now? What shapes,
textures and shades of light and dark colours
do you notice around you? Perhaps there are
some colours in your environment that capture
your attention. Allow your mind to go to them.
Select whichever pen or pencil you are drawn
to in this moment and begin to colour. Notice
the crisp, white page and the black lines of the
picture before you. Drink in what you perceive,
moment by moment, and absorb what you enjoy.
Close your eyes for a few seconds and open them anew.
You may notice things that you did not see before.

'Wherever you go,
go with all your heart.'

Confucius

Mindfulness of
the Body

Take this time to become aware of your posture.
You may wish to adopt an alert yet comfortable
sitting position with both of your feet on the
floor. You are grounded in this moment. Notice
how your eyes move as they explore the pattern
before you. Observe your arm moving as you
colour, and your hand as it holds the pen or
pencil that you have chosen. Become aware
of your breath filling your lungs and chest as
you breathe and create. Your mind and body
are deeply connected in these moments.

A Mindful Moment

In this moment, I am whole.

In the Silence

Choose an environment that feels peaceful for you. One that is free from background noise, people talking, demands and interruptions. Turn off your mobile phone and notice how the silence sounds. Just listen. What can you hear? Register and allow any sounds that you perceive to wash over you, and tune in to your experience of this moment. Mindfully listen to your breathing. Notice the sounds that your pen or pencil makes when you pick it up and place it on the paper. Listen to yourself colouring, and notice when your mind speaks. You are the silent observer of your experience. Allow your thoughts to come and go while you immerse yourself in colouring. There is peace for you here.

Freedom to Be

In this time, in this space, you are invited to mindfully *be*. There is no pressure on you here and there are no expectations. There is no 'right' and no 'wrong' way to colour the pattern before you. You can choose which colours you use. You can choose how long to colour for. You can decide how you colour, and you can set your own pace. Inhabit each moment as it unfolds, and allow your mind the freedom to simply be. Become absorbed and immersed in your own experience of colouring.

'To see a World in a
grain of sand,
And a Heaven in a
wild flower,
Hold Infinity in the
palm of your hand,
And Eternity in an hour.'

William Blake

Mindfulness of Sensations

Take this moment to notice any sensations within your body right now. Observe where each feeling is and acknowledge its presence. Watch as sensations come and go and change. See if you can observe them with curiosity and openness, without wanting or needing things to be different from how they are right now. As you breathe gently, in and out, see if you can make space for these sensations. Allow them to be here with you while you colour, just as they are, and expand your awareness around them.

Reflections:

A Mindful Moment

I can observe the
sensations that I feel, and
I can see past them.

A Colouring Meditation

Settle in a comfortable place and smile at your decision to take this time for yourself. This is for you. Study the picture that you will colour and really look at it. When you are ready, select your palette and begin to colour mindfully. Breathe into your experience of colouring each contour, and see if you can use all of your five senses to savour each moment as it unfolds. If your mind wanders, simply note where it has gone and gently escort it back to the present moment with kindness and patience. As your pen or pencil connects with the page, feel yourself reconnect with the present moment. This is your sanctuary.

Contemplation

Before you colour the next pattern, take a moment
or two to reflect upon some of the things that
make this mindful colouring experience possible
for you. Allow your mind to be touched and
inspired by the existence of everyday objects like
paper, and coloured pens and pencils. Allow the
people that created these things to be in your
awareness, too. Take a moment to think about
the artist who designed the pattern that you are
choosing to colour, and marvel at the ability of
your mind and body to fill it with colour. Notice
how ordinary things can become extraordinary
when you contemplate them mindfully.

'Always hold fast to the present.
Every situation, indeed every
moment, is of infinite value,
for it is the representative
of a whole eternity.'

Johann Wolfgang von Goethe

Living in the Moment

Pause in this moment and notice your breathing. With each breath, you are creating space for yourself to be – just as you are. In this space, you are inviting your inner world and outer world to be here with you now – just as they are. Immerse yourself in colouring whenever you wish. If you notice that you have drifted off into your thoughts, patiently escort your mind back to your experience of colouring. Reclaim now for yourself and watch it unfold in colour, moment by moment.

A Mindful Moment

Colour in the now.

Observing Change

Observe your experience of colouring this pattern, moment by moment. Notice each small change that occurs with every new mark that you make and every colour that you add. Witness the picture evolve as you fill it with colour, and acknowledge your role in creating the changes that you see. See if you can be aware of your internal landscape as it changes, too. Observe your thoughts and allow them to come and go. Make space for your emotions while you colour, too, and notice if they change, without judgement. Savour each moment and embrace each 'now'.

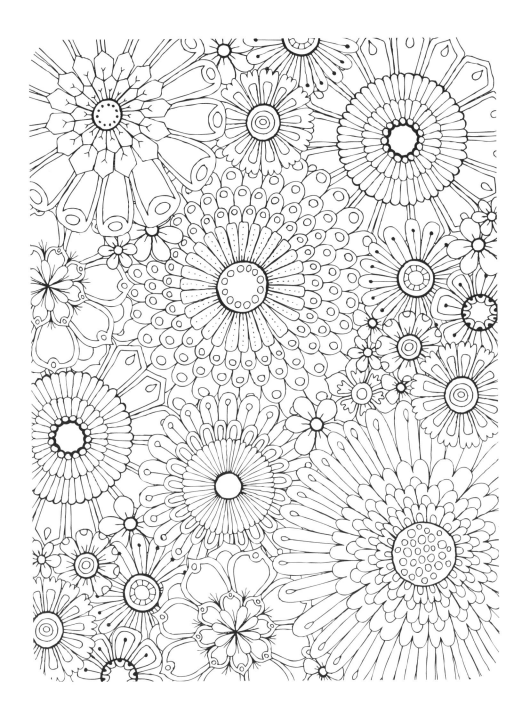

Mindfulness for Self-awareness

Witness the thoughts that come and go from your mind
while you are colouring. Write them down and return
your attention to the present moment. Practise being
the observer of your thoughts and notice the stillness
underneath them. Feel your feelings and invite them to
be here with you now. They offer insight into your well-
being. Acknowledge and accept them as best you can.
Set aside some time to respond to your thoughts
later with kindness and curiosity. Did they contain
judgements or impulses? Were they helpful? Were
they true? How were they linked to your emotions?
Give yourself a little distance from your thoughts
and see what you can learn about yourself.

'It is in your power to withdraw yourself whenever you desire. Perfect tranquillity within consists in the good ordering of the mind, the realm of your own.'

Marcus Aurelius

Drop Your Anchor

You may wish to practise this now, before you colour. Close your eyes, if you like, and place both your feet on the floor. Breathe in through your nose for the count of four, and out through your mouth for the count of six. Do this several times. Breathe in for four, and out for six. If you drift off into your thoughts, gently escort your mind back to the present moment and anchor yourself there. Notice the feeling of your feet on the floor, your body as it moves with your breath, and the experience of gently breathing. You have the capacity to soothe and ground yourself in times of stress.

A Mindful Moment

My body and breath can anchor me now.

Letting Go

In this moment, there is freedom. You do not need to expect, react, hold on or strive. Simply allow the process of colouring to reveal itself to you, moment by moment. Allow your thoughts and feelings the freedom to come and go as they wish. Let them leave, and observe them as they pass by. You can explore them with perspective and clarity later if you want to. In this moment, you are choosing to embrace your experience of colouring.

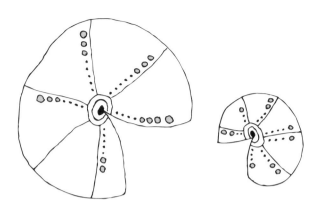

I choose to respond, not react.

Reflections:

Remembering Mindfulness

Being mindful takes practice, compassion and
patience. In order to practise it, we need to
remember that mindfulness is here for us to
use in our everyday lives. This can be easy to
forget and we can slip back into our old ways
of being. If you like mindfulness, then make
a conscious choice to try to hold it in your
heart and mind. If you forget about it and
then remember, be mindful! Offer yourself
compassion and then reconnect with yourself
in the present moment. Start now. Contemplate
what mindfulness is and put your learning into
practice as you colour this final picture.
Mindfulness is here for you as long as you are here.

Continuing Your Journey With Mindfulness

Some useful resources:

Alidina, S. *Mindfulness for Dummies*. John Wiley & Sons Ltd, 2010.

André, C. *Mindfulness: 25 Ways to Live in the Moment Through Art*. Ebury Publishing, 2014.

Kabat-Zinn, J. *Wherever You Go, There You Are: Mindfulness Meditation in Everyday Life*. Hyperion Books, 1994.

Nhat Hanh T. *The Miracle of Mindfulness: An Introduction to the Practice of Meditation*, trans. Mobi Ho, Rider Books, 1991.

Penman, D. and Williams, M. G. *Mindfulness: A Practical Guide to Finding Peace in a Frantic World*. Hachette Digital, Little Brown Book Group, 2011.

Williams, M., Teasdale, J., Segal, Z., and Kabat-Zinn, J. *The Mindful Way Through Depression: Freeing Yourself From Chronic Unhappiness*. The Guilford Press, 2007.

For more information about what mindfulness is, how to do it and some brilliant free guided meditations (in 'Resources') go to:
www.franticworld.com

A word of caution:

It is important to state that a small proportion of people find the practice of mindfulness meditation too emotionally challenging. If this is your experience, then now may not be the right time for you to practise mindfulness without suitable support. It may be helpful to speak to a supportive mental health professional about your thoughts and feelings instead. Mindfulness will be here when the time is right for you.

About the Author

Dr Sarah Jane Arnold is a Chartered Counselling Psychologist. In her private practice she works with people experiencing life issues and specific mental health difficulties, to enhance their well-being via integrative, mindfulness-informed psychological therapy.

Sarah lives in Brighton, in the UK, with her partner, Mine, their dog, Oprah, and Priscilla the bearded dragon.